Elevation For Revelation

By

S.Y.Elliott

TABLE OF CONTENTS

About The Book

Elevation For Revelation is an insightful and creative approach to Scriptures. This book will cause you to move from level to dimension

Galatians 2:2 KJV: And I went up by revelation

Paul went up by Revelation not by education, connection, money, fame, social media, influence or popularity. But he went up by revelation. The devil can stop your education but the devil cannot stop your revelation. Nothing changes a situation like revelation. Read this book. The sky will not be a limit. The sky will be a cushion for you to go to another dimension. I release the Star Trek anointing, you will go to a place where no man has ever gone before. Remember you're on your way up by revelation and nothing can stop you.

Ephesians 1:17-18 KJV

That the God of our Lord Jesus Christ, the Father of glory, may give unto you the spirit of wisdom and revelation in the knowledge of him: [18] The eyes of your understanding being enlightened; that ye may know what is the hope of his calling, and what the riches of the glory of his inheritance in the saints,

DEDICATION

I dedicate this book to my wife Maude for being a virtuous, as a good thing that have caused me to obtain favor.

ANOINTED TO THE BONES

2 Kings 13

As we look briefly at the life of Elisha, one that was anointed with the double portion. He followed Elijah faithfully and his master became his father.

In 2 Kings chapter 13:14

Elisha is anointed and sick. You can be anointed and sick, anointed and depressed, anointed and oppressed, anointed and face eviction, anointed and downcast, anointed and divorced, anointed and broke. A lot of people get it confused and get it twisted and think when you are anointed, you don't go through problems and challenges. That is so far from the truth.

The anointing on your life will attract problems and challenges. As a matter of fact, the devil is not fighting you, because of where you are, what you drive, where you live, the clothes you wear and the degree you have. The devil is fighting you because of the anointing on your life.

America went to Iraq to find weapons of mass destruction. Up til now, they have not found weapons of mass destruction.

The war in Iraq was not over weapons. It was over oil. The enemy is fighting you because of the anointing you carry. America went to Libya, not because of Qaddafi but because of the control of oil. You must understand you are anointed and the anointed will attract trouble and challenges.

Elisha is anointed with a double portion and he is sick. I don't want you to feel less anointed because you are going through problems, challenges and difficulties

Psalm 34:19 KJV

[19] Many are the afflictions of the righteous: but the Lord delivereth him out of them all.

Elisha dies but his bones are still anointed. You are not truly anointed until you can get past your flesh.

Romans 8:5-8 KJV

[5] For they that are after the flesh do mind the things of the flesh; but they that are after the Spirit the things of the Spirit. [6] For to be carnally minded is death; but to be spiritually minded is life and peace. [7] Because the carnal mind is enmity against God: for it is not subject to the law of God, neither indeed can be. [8] So then they that are in the flesh cannot please God.

Galatians 5:16 KJV

[16] This I say then, Walk in the Spirit, and ye shall not fulfil the lust of the flesh.

You are not truly anointed until you can get past your ego.

John 12:24 KJV

[24] Verily, verily, I say unto you, Except a corn of wheat fall into the ground and die, it abideth alone: but if it dies, it bringeth forth much fruit.

Your ego, pride, jealousy, bitterness, and unforgiveness will hinder your anointing. The anointing in your life will not be in full operation until you are dead to yourself. Not my will but yours be done.

Bones represent structure. Without your bones you will be like a jellyfish. You will be like jello. You will have no structure.

Wherever you have no structure, you have no success. Every successful thing in life has a structure. Your anointing is not in full operation until you have structure and order in your life.

Ezekiel 37, God did not release his spirit, until the bones were in order.

Isaiah 38:1 KJV

[1] In those days was Hezekiah sick unto death. And Isaiah the prophet the son of Amoz came unto him, and said unto him, Thus saith the Lord, Set thine house in order: for thou shalt die, and not live.

God sent the prophet Isaiah to the house of Hezekiah and told him to set his house in order. His house was out of order. And God said he was going to die. Bones represent order.

God asked the Prophet Ezekiel can these bones live? Can you live without a man? Can you live without popping pills? Can you live without depending on the government? Can you live without being depressed? Can you live without depending on people?

Let's look at "John 19:32-33 KJV"

[32] Then came the soldiers, and broke the legs of the first, and of the other which was crucified with him. [33] But when they came to Jesus, and saw that he was dead already, they brake not his legs:

They broke the other criminal's bones and not the bones of Jesus because he's anointed to the bone. Somebody needs to thank the Lord. The things that should have destroyed you, stopped you, hindered you, did not happen. It didn't destroy you. It didn't kill you. It didn't make you bitter. It didn't make you sad because you are anointed to the bone. They wanted to break his bones so that he would not be able to walk or stand. He would not be able to walk in power, do good and heal those oppressed with the devil (Acts 10:38).

Elijah is dead. I declare, you will not die. You will live to declare the glory of the Lord. Psalm 118:17

John 11:4 KJV

[4] When Jesus heard that, he said, This sickness is not unto

death, but for the glory of God, that the Son of God might be glorified thereby.

2 Kings, chapter 13. The enemy came in the spring. Why is this important? Because it's harvest time. You are close to a miracle. You are close to your blessing. You are close to your breakthrough.

The enemy always comes to steal, to kill, and to destroy so You don't get your harvest

Galatians 6:9 KJV

[9] And let us not be weary in well doing: for in due season we shall reap, if we faint not.

“Once while some Israelites were burying a man, suddenly they saw a band of raiders; so they threw the man’s body into Elisha’s tomb. When the body touched Elisha’s bones, the man came to life and stood up on his feet.” 2 Kings 13:21 NIV

We don't know his name, but he's dead. They threw him in the tomb. A lot of people will throw you away because they think you are not qualified, that you are not all that, you don’t meet their qualifications, you're not part of the clique. But God will never throw you away. Preachers and prophets and fake friends will throw you away and let you down, but God We never let you down.

Psalm 27:10 KJV

[10] When my father and my mother forsake me, then the Lord will take me up.

Hebrews 13:5 KJV

[5] for he hath said, I will never leave thee, nor forsake thee.

When his body touched the bones of Elisha, he got up. Why? Because Elisha was anointed to the bone. Tell the Enemy, you can attack my body, my house, my mind, my children, my family, but not my bones. I'm anointed to the bone.

Jeremiah 20:9 KJV

[9] Then I said, I will not make mention of him, nor speak any more in his name. But his word was in mine heart as a burning fire shut up in my bones, and I was weary with forbearing, and I could not stay.

But the reason I'm still worshiping, the reason I'm still praying, the reason I'm still loving God is because I'm anointed to the bone. My anointing is not in church, not in a house, clothes, money, not in beauty, not in cars, not in education. I'm anointed to the bones. That's why small stuff doesn't bother me. The devil can't stop me. Haters can't block me. Depression can't hinder me.

Witches can't get a hold on me because I'm anointed to the bones. I eat demons for lunch. God, turn my witches into sandwiches. They lied on me, scandalized my name, walked out on me, and took my job. I will still be anointed because I'm anointed to the bone. My honey may be running. My money may be funny. My children may be acting up. But the reason I'm not crying myself to sleep, the reason I'm not in the mental institution, the reason I'm not in a fetal position, the reason I'm not in the corner, counting my fingers coming up with 15 Instead of 10, not trying to jump off the Brooklyn Bridge, not smoking Newport, not high on crack is because I'm anointed to the bones.

In my sleep, I'm anointed. Cars or no cars. Married or not. Having money or not, house or not. I'm still anointed. Even when family members let me down, friends talk about me, the doctors give me a negative report, they give me a pink slip on my job, or cut my hours. I'm still anointed. You can take the job. You can take cars, clothes, money, and houses. A man can walk out of my life. My anointing will still be intact. Because my anointing is not in stuff, it's not in cars, not in clothes, inot in money. It is in my bones. You are anointed to the bones and the devil can't do nothing about it. Corona can't stop you. Demons can't break you. Witches can't stand you because you are too anointed. You are anointed to the bones.

Psalm 105:15 KJV

[15] Saying, Touch not mine anointed, and do my prophets no harm.

CRUSH THE SNAKE'S HEAD

Genesis 3:15 KJV

[15] And I will put enmity between thee and the woman, and between thy seed and her seed; it shall bruise thy head, and thou shalt bruise his heel.

Luke 10:19 KJV

[19] Behold, I give unto you power to tread on serpents and scorpions, and over all the power of the enemy: and nothing shall by any means hurt you.

You have more power than the devil. You have more power than sickness. You have more power than pain. You have more power than witches. You have more power than demonic and satanic forces. You have to learn how to use your power and authority.

He said nothing shall by any means hurt you

The word nothing means "no thing." No demon, no devil. No pain, no disappointment. Nothing shall by any means hurt you.

Jeremiah 1:10 KJV

[10] See, I have this day set thee over the nations and over the kingdoms, to root out, and to pull down, and to destroy, and to throw down, to build, and to plant.

"But the Lord is with me like a mighty warrior; so my persecutors will stumble and not prevail.

They will fail and be thoroughly disgraced; their dishonor will never be forgotten." Jeremiah 20:11 NIV

In Genesis three, God speaks to the serpent. First, before Adam and Eve, you have to learn how to speak to the devil, to the enemy, to witches and wizards, to demonic powers. You have to let the devil know the blood of Jesus is upon you.

You can't stop my family, my progress, my anointing, my marriage, my ministry, my business. Speak to the snake. Crush the snake. Don't sleep with the snake.

Don't text, don't eat with snakes or befriend snakes. You have to learn how to crush the head of every snake in Jesus Name

Too many Christians are sleeping with the enemy and talking with snakes. That's the mistake Eve made talking with the snake and entertaining the snake. You have to let the snake -- the devil -- know you can't touch my life. You can't touch my family. You can't touch my anointing.

You can't touch my money. You can't touch my health, my marriage, my daughter and my son.

Psalm 105:15 KJV

[15] Saying, Touch not mine anointed, and do my prophets no harm.

Do not play with a snake. Do not manage the devil, damage the devil. God said, I will put enmity between you and the woman. I will put a wall, I will put a divide between you and my church. You can never get her back. She belongs to me. Whatever the enemy has done and all the mistakes you have made, God wants you back. He wants to love you. He wants to protect you. He wants to watch over you with jealous eyes. Just like the prodigal father, when the son returns, Father, I'm not worthy to be called your son. Make me your servant. I have sinned against heaven, and I've sinned against you. The father opened his arms. The father receives the son, empowers the son, gives him a robe, gives him a ring, and gives him sandals. That's what makes the enemy mad. With all the mess ups and all the sin, the Father still loves us

After Adam and Eve messed up and ate the fruit, God told him not to eat, Satan thought he had won. He thought God would never speak to Adam again. But after Adam messed up, God came and called Adam.

Genesis 3:9 KJV

[9] And the Lord God called unto Adam, and said unto him, Where art thou?

Even when I'm out of the will of God I can still hear his voice. Some of us have not done everything right. Some of us have messed up, but we still hear his voice. He has taken our mess and turned it into a message. You've taken our mistake and turn it into a miracle. He can pick up a prophet from the projects. God can take somebody on crack, to crack the code and the head of the devil. He can take a prostitute and turn her into an evangelist. He can take a liar and turn him into a father of all nations. God calls Adam after he messes up. God is calling you. You may have missed it. You may have fallen, you may have done something that is not pleasing to God, but he still loves you. That's why you cannot mess with snakes. You cannot eat with them. You cannot sleep with them.

I don't care where they live, what they drive, what they wear, how much money they make. You have to crush the head of every snake.

I will put an enmity between your seed and her seed. Your seed and the seed of the devil. Satan has children. Demons and agents working overtime for him. Some of them are on your job. Some of them are in your family.

Some of them are around you. You talk, text, and communicate with them. God has empowered your seed with the gift of spiritual warfare to break and destroy demonic powers, influences, plot and plans of the enemy. Our children, sons and daughters, will not go to prison and will not do drugs, alcohol. The police will not touch them. Our daughters will not be side chicks, or baby mamas. Our daughters will not be on an abortion table. They will never drop out of school. Our sons will not spend a night in jail, or in rehab. They will not be confused about their sexuality, their identity. They will not be on any behavior modification medicine, they will not lose their self esteem.

They will crush the head of the enemy.

Genesis 22:17 KJV

[17] That in blessing I will bless thee, and in multiplying I will multiply thy seed as the stars of the heaven, and as the sand which is upon the sea shore; and thy seed shall possess the gate of his enemies;

God told the snake, you will bruise his heel, the bottom of his foot. When your heel is in pain it may stop you from walking. You will walk on crutches, but it will not kill you. The enemy will cause pain. The enemy will attack. The enemy will do his worst, but it will not kill you .

Isaiah 54:17 KJV

[17] No weapon that is formed against thee shall prosper; and every tongue that shall rise against thee in judgment thou shalt condemn. This is the heritage of the servants of the Lord, and their righteousness is of me, saith the Lord.

You may be in pain, but you will still praise God. I'm in pain, but I'm still worshiping. I'm in pain, but I'm still giving. I'm still loving God. I'm still flourishing in my business. I'm on an assignment. I'm in pain, but God is watching over me. I'm in pain, but I refuse to give up.

Why is he attacking my heel? Because the devil is under my feet. I'm stepping on every demon. I'm crushing every evil spirit, every witch, every poverty, every depression, every setback, every delay, every confusion. I'm crushing the head of the snake. The reason why you have to praise God is because anytime you step, you crush the head of the devil. The reason why you have to praise God is because the blood of Jesus is all over you, from the crown of your head to the soles of your feet.

And as you crush the head of the serpent, you will step and possess new places, new testimonies, new territories, new houses, new relationships, new opportunities, new songs, and a new bill of health. Declare I'm stepping in a new neighborhood, a new school, a new dimension because I have crushed the head of every snake. Hallelujah, Amen.

Devil You Made One Mistake

In Daniel chapter three, we find a king full of himself and making a golden image. He said everybody should bow and worship this image. You have to be careful of images. Romans chapter 12 verse one and two. The image of this world can contaminate and pollute your relationship with God. Also, you have to be very careful not to be full of yourself. I'll be very careful with people who are full of themselves

Romans 12 three. Everybody bows to this image but not the three Hebrew boys. They refused to bow. They refuse to bend. You refuse to compromise

You must purpose in your heart not to defile yourself. Not to blend in, but to stand out. Not to compromise.

Exodus 11 verse seven. You must be known for your excellence and your difference. The fact that everybody is doing it does not make it right. Some see that everybody is dressing half naked, showing the body parts because it's a new fashion.

As a child of God you have to present your bodies as a living sacrifice. Refuse to bow and refuse to compromise and refuse to sin.

Refuse to do what others are doing. First Corinthians seven, verse one.

In Daniel chapter one, the king changes their names. The first name is Hananiah. It means beloved of God. He changed the name, but he never changed the love of God, their commitment, their dedication, their passion, or their spirit.

They can change your position, your wages, and your clothes. You can even change the car you drive, the house you live in. You can move from one community to the next. Change your location. But I pray you will never change your passion, your love, your commitment to God.

They changed his name to Shadrach, which means the farm God. But thank God His love for God did not change.

The second Hebrew boy name is Mishael, which means who is like God. That should be our greatest desire. I want to be like God. Before the left Egypt, God told them to kill the land and eat the whole land.

Who is the limb of Jesus? It's the eye, the leg, the feet, the intestine, the heart. So you can see like me, talk like me, walk like me, and understand the game in the workings.

First John chapter four verse one.

They named Mishael like the sun god, but the Hebrew boy said I want to be like God. Don't be like Beyonce, Jay Z, Rihanna, or Cardi B. Be yourself. Be like God.

The third Hebrew boy named is Azariah, which means the LORD is my help. Psalm chapter 121. Psalm 34, verse five, the Lord is our help. When nobody can help us, God is my help.

When everybody refuses to help us, God is my help. So chapter four, verse 12 to 16. The changes lead to a ban and they are told to serve a false god. But he said because God is my help I will not serve it. For God, I will not serve money. I will not serve fashion. I will not serve drugs. I will not serve alcohol because God Is my help.

God will allow you to go through chapters in your life where the people you thought were going to help you are not here to help you, stand with you or pray with you. They will never be around. So your hope, your trust and your faith can be in God and God alone. God gets all the glory. At the end of the day, it will not be about your mother, your supervisor, a man, or a woman, but it will be God and God alone.

Because they refused to bow, the King got angry and said, I'm going to give you one more opportunity to bow to my image. The Hebrew boys said, you don't have to waste your time. We will not bow. Even if God does not deliver us.

I'm going to be faithful. The King told them to make the burning furnace seven times hotter. Seven is the number of completion and perfection. It can get no hotter than this. This is the hottest. That will completely destroy the Hebrew boys. The king asked for the strongest men to throw the Hebrew boys into the fire. Whenever the enemy is coming after anointed people, he comes strong. He comes well prepared because the anointing on your life is so unique, so powerful. The enemy sends the strongest to step in to destroy you.

The men that threw the Hebrew Boys in the fire, die from the fire.

Can I prophesy to you? Those that throw you in the fire, lied on you, criticize you, and scandalize will catch fire and die themselves before throwing them in the fire. They tie their hands so that they wouldn't lift up their hands and praise God. They tied their feet so the wouldn't dance and walk in the authority that God had given them. But they made one mistake. They should have covered and shut their mouths.

Worshiper know how to shout in the fire, in pain and in disappointment. When everything is against a worshiper, a worshiper can lift his hands and praise God in the midst of a storm.

They are from Judah.

Judah represents praise. You can never keep a praiser or worshiper depressed, confused, or suppressed. When praises go up, blessing, deliverance, anointing, and power come down.

Their hands and feet were tied so they were not standing on their feet but they were laying on the ground. I can tell You are an authentic worshipper. You may not be in church. You may not be out at a gospel concert.

An authentic worshiper can worship God in the midst of the fire. They open their mouth to worship God

And the things that held them tie,d held them in captivity, held them bound, the thing that incapacitated them, when they begin to worship have to break off of them.

The king was amazed. He said didn't we put three men in the fire? I see four. And the fourth one looks like the Son of God.

The devil made a mistake. He may take the car, take the

clothes, take the money, take the relationship, but never allow him to take your praise.

Psalm 22:3

John 4:23 and 24

Worship brings God in the place. When you and I worship God will show up every time.

I tell people I don't want to be a great preacher, a great teacher, a great apostle. I want to be a great worshipper.

God said David is the man after my heart because David was a worshiper.

Psalm 34, verse one,

Something that is very interesting, in chapter one, the Hebrew boys purpose in their heart, not to defile themselves. Not to drink alcohol, but to only eat vegetables and drink water. Why is that important? If they had drunk alcohol, the fire would have destroyed them. They would have been incinerated. When we look at the bottle of alcohol, it says it is flammable. Nothing causes a fire to blaze like alcohol. If alcohol had been in the system the fire would have destroyed them.

It is Important you purpose in your heart. Now to defy yourself not to do what others are doing.

Psalm 119, verse nine and 11.

Psalm chapter one, do not defy yourself, live for God. It may not be popular, but God has never been known to be popular. No one anointed you to be average.

He anointed you to stand out.

The king said, I see four men walking in the fire, and the fourth one looks like the Son of God. Remember, Jesus was not supposed to show up until Matthew.

But for a worshipper, Jesus will show up early.

God is showing up early in your chapter to change your story.

To change your life,

To change your family to change your situation. First one is six.

The furnace door was not closed. The door was open even in the midst of fire. God opened the door. They called the name in the fire and three of them came out.

Verse 27,

You can tell you are a worshiper. You don't look, smell, or dress like what you've been through. Don't make the mistake the devil made.

Don’t stop worshipping God.

Don't stop praising him.

A worshiper will always get God's attention. The wall will show up.

Be on the fence of worship.

Authentic worshipers can attract heaven always in your life

I'M COVERED

Grasshoppers cannot defend themselves. But they eat poisonous plants and then put it on themselves so that lizards cannot eat them. Every now and again, you have to thank God for what is in you. You have to thank God for the blood of Jesus that is on you that the enemy cannot touch you.

Genesis 6:5 KJV

[5] And God saw that the wickedness of man was great in the earth, and that every imagination of the thoughts of his heart was only evil continually.

Their thoughts are filled with evil. A lot of people judge people based on their actions. But God judges base on the thoughts

Matthew 15:17-19 KJV

[17] Do not ye yet understand, that whatsoever entereth in at the mouth goeth into the belly, and is cast out into the draught? [18] But those things which proceed out of the mouth come forth from the heart; and they defile the man. [19] For out of

the heart proceed evil thoughts, murders, adulteries, fornications, thefts, false witness, blasphemies:

Jeremiah 17:9-10 KJV

[9] The heart is deceitful above all things, and desperately wicked: who can know it? [10] I the Lord search the heart, I try the reins, even to give every man according to his ways, and according to the fruit of his doings.

We cannot see what people are thinking. The fact you thought about it is more dangerous than those who actually do it.

Matthew 5:28 KJV

[28] But I say unto you, That whosoever looketh on a woman to lust after her hath committed adultery with her already in his heart.

Just looking with lust and not touching is committing adultery

God calls Noah to build an ark. Noah is not an engineer. He doesn't have a builder's license. He has never built an ark before. God will call you to do things that do not match your background, what you are not qualified for. You have no experience, you have no formal training. Things that don’t make sense. But that's how you know it is from God.

1 Corinthians 1:27-29 KJV

[27] But God hath chosen the foolish things of the world to

confound the wise; and God hath chosen the weak things of the world to confound the things which are mighty; [28] And base things of the world, and things which are despised, hath God chosen, yea, and things which are not, to bring to nought things that are: [29] That no flesh should glory in his presence.

He doesn't call the qualified but he qualifies those he calls.

At 600 years old, God calls Noah. You are not too old for the call of God or for God to use you

Nelson Mandela was 77years old when he became president of South Africa. Colonel Sanders, founder of KFC and Mary Kay were both well over 50 when they started their business careers. Remember, you're never too old to be what you could have been.

The first instruction God gave Noah was to cut down a tree. Remember, Jesus was crucified on a tree. The Ark is shaped like a coffin. Sometimes God will put us in situations that look like it will kill us. But he puts you in there to make you strong. He will allow people to say things and do things to you. The very people you thought had your back. The people you thought were there to support you, are the ones trying to destroy you. But you will not die, you will get stronger in the place of pain, persecution and criticism.

Psalm 23:5 KJV

[5] Thou preparest a table before me in the presence of mine enemies: thou anointest my head with oil; my cup runneth over.

He never said your enemies would eat with you. Your enemies will watch you eat, watch God bless you. Watch you get a house, get married, get a promotion, etc. Some of us have been through things that should have killed us. But thank God we are still alive. Most of us have slept and had unprotected sex, but no HIV, no STDs. Some of us smoked, but no cancer, drank alcohol and had no liver problems. You have to thank God.

That's why sometimes I believe God is confused by our actions. Because we are alive and won't praise God. We have hands and won't clap, feet and won't dance for Him, etc.

Coronavirus didn't kill you. The divorce did not take you to a mental institution. People walk out of your life and you're still in your sound mind. How do you need somebody to beg you to praise God? You need a praise team, a prophet or a cheerleader to give God praise.

Something inside of us has to say, "because I have breath, I'm gonna praise."

Psalm 150:6 KJV

[6] Let every thing that hath breath praise the Lord. Praise ye the Lord.

It took Noah 120 years to finish the ark. Jesus was on the cross for six hours. What God is going to do in your life will amaze and shock people. People will wonder how what took others years will take you months. What took others months will take you weeks. What took other weeks will take you days, God is going to accelerate your progress.

In verse 16, The Ark is three dimensional. Upper Deck. Middle Deck, and the lower deck.

There are three arks in the Bible.

The first Ark. The Ark of Noah, which represents salvation.

The second Ark. The Ark of Moses, saved from the decree to kill every baby under the age of two years old.

The third Ark, the Ark of the Covenant,

Hebrews 9:4 KJV

[4] Which had the golden censer, and the ark of the covenant overlaid round about with gold, wherein was the golden pot that had manna, and Aaron's rod that budded, and the tables of the covenant;

Genesis 7:1 KJV

[1] And the Lord said unto Noah, Come thou and all thy house into the ark; for thee have I seen righteous before me in this generation.

God called Noah into the ark. Noah got the call of God. But his whole family came in the ark. Once you understand the call of God on your life, those connected to you will be blessed, get a breakthrough, favor, open doors and opportunities because of you.

You are not anointed to be stuck up, selfish, arrogant and alone. But you are anointed to bring your whole family into wealth, into favor into the kingdom of God.

The Ark, only had one door

John 10:9 KJV

[9] I am the door: by me if any man enter in, he shall be saved, and shall go in and out, and find pasture.

There is only one way to eternal life and that way is Jesus.

John 14:6 KJV

[6] Jesus saith unto him, I am the way, the truth, and the life: no man cometh unto the Father, but by me.

Ephesians 4:4-6 KJV

[4] There is one body, and one Spirit, even as ye are called in
one hope of your calling; [5] One Lord, one faith, one baptism,
[6] One God and Father of all, who is above all, and through
all, and in you all.

The Ark also had one window and the window was not on the side. But the window was on the top, because God did not want them to see the stuff they had lost. He wanted them to look to heaven, where their help came from (Psalms 121)

Your help does not come from around. Your help is not from your job, your spouse, the government or social society. Your help comes from heaven. (Psalms 34:5"). Too many times, we put our trust in people, in the government, and in the system.

The system, the government, and people will fail you. God never fails.

Hebrews 6:10 KJV

[10] For God is not unrighteous to forget your work and labour of love, which ye have shewed toward his name, in that ye have ministered to the saints, and do minister.

The flood caused Noah to move. You have to thank God for the flood.

Sometimes we are stuck, complacent and relaxed, and we get comfortable. But because of problems and situations, they begin to move. The songwriter sings, if I never had a problem. I never knew God could solve them through it at all. I've learned to trust in Jesus. When people hurt you, walk out on you, scandalize your name, criticize you, it moves you to another dimension. You have to thank God for the storm, you have to thank God for those haters, because your haters became your elevators.

Genesis 6:14 KJV

[14] Make thee an ark of gopher wood; rooms shalt thou make in the ark, and shalt pitch it within and without with pitch.

He covered the ark with pitch so that no water could get in. But God covers you and I, not with pitch, but with the blood of Jesus. Thank God for the blood. Thank God for the cross. The cross without the blood is just wood. When Noah got out of the ark, he built an altar and sacrificed burnt offerings and when God smelled the aroma, God said He would never destroy the Earth again. We have to sacrifice.

The sacrifice is thanksgiving and praise. Because in the midst of the mess, coronavirus Delta variance plagues and diseases, He covers us. Our families are covered. Children cover mothers and fathers. He covers us from the virus, from witches, from the plague, from destruction, from perplexities, from sicknesses, from accidents and incidents. Thank God. You are covered

ITS IN YOUR MOUTH

Matthew 17:24-27

Jesus is in Capernaum and the collectors of the tax came to Peter and wanted to find out if Jesus paid the temple tax. They were not talking about the Roman taxes, but wanted to find out about the temple tax. Notice they did not have a problem paying the temple tax for the upkeep of the house of God. It is so interesting that nowadays people don't have a problem paying government taxes, but have a problem paying tithes in church. Something is wrong when we have a greater reverence for the government than for God and his house

Matthew 6:33 KJV

[33] But seek ye first the kingdom of God, and his righteousness; and all these things shall be added unto you.

Isaiah 9:6 KJV

[6] For unto us a child is born, unto us a son is given: and the government shall be upon his shoulder: and his name shall be called Wonderful, Counsellor, The mighty God, The everlasting

Father, The Prince of Peace.

"The government will be upon his shoulder"

They did not ask Peter about his taxes, only Jesus. When you are anointed, when you have the call of God on your life and you're on an assignment, people will be all in your business. They don't even know you, but want to be into you to see how they can hurt you. And Jesus had no problem with paying his taxes, his dues. Jesus will pay the bill. He will pay your bills. Some of us have more bills than money, mortgages, car notes, Student Loans. But when you trust God, He will pay the bill.

A lot of people don't know how much you had to pay to get here. Don't know the nights you stayed up all night, fasting and praying. You gave when you didn't have enough. You had to go to work and school. Take care of your parents and your children. A lot of people want success but no sacrifice, crowns but no Cross, testimony, but no test. Victory but no battle, triumph but no trial. You have to pay the price. Not just for clothes, cars, and houses, but you have to pay the price to be happy, to sleep at night, to have peace of mind, etc.

Jesus asked Peter who should pay taxes ? He's talking about the kingdom because he's a son of the king.

He said who does the king or the people of the earth collect taxes from, their own sons or others? And Peter said the others. He said there are certain things we shouldn't have to go through. You should not have to be broke, sick, depressed and lonely, delayed, rejected, etc.

But the reason why we go through these things is to make us strong, better and wiser

ArchBishop Duncan Williams said, “challenges are for the living and not the dead”

Psalm 30:5 KJV

[5] For his anger endureth but a moment; in his favour is life: weeping may endure for a night, but joy cometh in the morning.

Psalm 119:71 KJV

[71] It is good for me that I have been afflicted; that I might learn thy statutes.

That's why some of us don't have any regrets. But we thank God for the experiences.

I'm stronger, I'm better. And I'm thankful for the mountain. And even the valleys. Jesus said, I shouldn't have to pay taxes. I'm a son of the king. As a child of God, you shouldn't have to be broke, depressed, stressed, living from paycheck to paycheck. But challenges are not for the dead. They are for the living.

Jesus said because we don't want to offend people, we'll go the extra mile. Because I don't want any drama, I don't want to argue, I don't want to fight, I don't want to cuss, I will just do it. He said we don't want to offend anybody.

Poverty is offensive. People you don't want to talk to have the audacity to talk to you, call you, question you, interrogate you. Poverty also brings public embarrassment. They ask Peter this question in public. I pray that after today God will deliver you from public embarrassment. The absence of money is the presence of unnecessary questions.

Your children ask you questions. Your credit card company, your mortgage company, family members, friends and coworkers ask you unnecessary question, people in department stores etc

Poverty also sponsors abnormality. People that are not supposed to talk to you begin to talk to you. People begin to disrespect you, call you names. You lose respect in the community sometimes even in the church.

In verse 27 Jesus gave Peter some keys that I want to give you to turn financial embarrassment into abundance.

He said go to the lake

A) you must follow directions.

Joshua 6:3-5 KJV

[3] And ye shall compass the city, all ye men of war, and go round about the city once. Thus shalt thou do six days. [4] And seven priests shall bear before the ark seven trumpets of rams' horns: and the seventh day ye shall compass the city seven times, and the priests shall blow with the trumpets. [5] And it shall come to pass, that when they make a long blast with the ram's horn, and when ye hear the sound of the trumpet, all the people shall shout with a great shout; and the wall of the city shall fall down flat, and the people shall ascend up every man straight before him.

God told the children of Israel to march around the walls of Jericho for seven days on the seventh day to march around the walls seven times. They followed instructions

Joshua 6:15-16 KJV

[15] And it came to pass on the seventh day, that they rose early about the dawning of the day, and compassed the city after the same manner seven times: only on that day they compassed the city seven times. [16] And it came to pass at the seventh time, when the priests blew with the trumpets, Joshua said unto the people, Shout; for the Lord hath given you the city.

Elisha gave the widow instructions

2 Kings 4:2-4 KJV

[2] And Elisha said unto her, What shall I do for thee? tell me, what hast thou in the house? And she said, Thine handmaid hath not any thing in the house, save a pot of oil. [3] Then he said,

Go, borrow thee vessels abroad of all thy neighbours, even empty vessels; borrow not a few. [4] And when thou art come in, thou shalt shut the door upon thee and upon thy sons, and shalt pour out into all those vessels, and thou shalt set aside that which is full.

Jesus gave the servants instructions

John 2:7 KJV

[7] Jesus saith unto them, Fill the waterpots with water. And they filled them up to the brim.

If you want to be blessed financially, you must follow directions.

B) You must obey instructions. Partial obedience is disobedience.

Deuteronomy 28:1-3 KJV[1] And it shall come to pass, if thou shalt hearken diligently unto the voice of the Lord thy God, to observe and to do all his commandments which I command thee this day, that the Lord thy God will set thee on high above all nations of the earth: [2] And all these blessings shall come on thee, and overtake thee, if thou shalt hearken unto the voice of the Lord thy God. [3] Blessed shalt thou be in the city, and blessed shalt thou be in the field.

Job 36:11 KJV

[11] If they obey and serve him, they shall spend their days in prosperity, and their years in pleasures.

1 Samuel 15:22b KJV

[22] to obey is better than sacrifice, and to hearken than the fat of rams.

Obey instruction

"""But so that we may not cause offense, go to the lake and throw out your line. Take the first fish you catch; open its mouth and you will find a four-drachma coin. Take it and give it to them for my tax and yours.""""

Matthew 17:27 NIV

He said throw your line. The line has a hook on it. You need a supernatural hook up. This season of your life God is going to hook you up with somebody that has resources, that can underwrite your ideas, your dream, your vision. He's going to hook you up with a prayer partner that can challenge and add to your spiritual life. He's going to hook you up with a prayer partner that isn't a prayer point. He's going to hook you up with a wife and not a knife. He's going to hook you up with a husband and not a hunchback. He's going to hook you up with a giver, not a taker. He's going to hook you up with somebody that brings joy in your life and not sorrow. He's gonna hook you up with somebody who will lift you up and not bring you down. As you're reading this book shout Lord Hook me up.

C) He said the first fish you catch. Take advantage of the first opportunity. A lot of us are waiting for the next, but God wants you to take advantage of the first. The first business, the first idea, the first dream, the first vision

Matthew 6:33 KJV

[33] But seek ye first the kingdom of God, and his righteousness; and all these things shall be added unto you.

D) Open its mouth and you will find money, "OPEN YOUR MOUTH." The money you need is in its mouth. I want you to hear me. Your money is not in the bank, it's in your mouth. Your blessing is in your mouth. Your healing, marriage, house, scholarship, citizenship, promotion is in your mouth.

Job 22:28 KJV

[28] Thou shalt also decree a thing, and it shall be established unto thee: and the light shall shine upon thy ways.

Psalm 107:2 KJV

[2] Let the redeemed of the Lord say so, whom he hath redeemed from the hand of the enemy;

Numbers 14:28 KJV

[28] Say unto them, As truly as I live, saith the Lord, as ye have spoken in mine ears, so will I do to you:

Proverbs 18:21 KJV

[21] Death and life are in the power of the tongue: and they that love it shall eat the fruit thereof.

Mark 11:23 KJV

[23] For verily I say unto you, That whosoever shall say unto this mountain, Be thou removed, and be thou cast into the sea; and shall not doubt in his heart, but shall believe that those things which he saith shall come to pass; he shall have whatsoever he saith.

Jesus never said go to the bank, your job, your credit card company etc. He said open the fish's mouth. The key to your financial prosperity is not in your job or your bank. It is in your mouth. Your confession is your possession. Stop confessing I'm broke, I don't have money, I will never make it, I'm suffering, things are hard. You have to learn how to open your mouth and speak positively. Your money is in your mouth. Your next car, your next house, your prosperity.

Your family deliverance is in your mouth.

I don't get sick. I can never be broke. I can never be down. Because I never confess I'm sick, and never confess I'm broke and never confess I'm down.

Creflo Dollar, years ago sent me a DVD. And while he's ministering, he said these words, “I will never be broke, not another day in my life.” That word left the television and entered my spirit. And I begin to confess. I will never be broke and I have never been broken since. What you confess is what you will possess. When you change your confession, you change your possession. Your miracle is in your mouth.

He said take the coin and gave it to them. Pay mine and yours. Connect with people that want to see you blessed. Connect with people I want to see you prosper, that want to see you do well. Stay away from selfish people.

They asked if Jesus paid taxes, but he didn't just pay his tax. He also paid for Peter because

Jesus will pay the bill. Remember it’s in your mouth

IT WONT TAKE THAT LONG

Jeremiah 29:28 KJV

[28] For therefore he sent unto us in Babylon, saying, This captivity is long: build ye houses, and dwell in them ; and plant gardens, and eat the fruit of them.

This captivity is long.....

We often hear it is going to happen now. God will do it. It won't take that long. This too will pass. What happens if it takes long or longer? What happens if your miracle and the blessing tarries and your answer is not instant?

Jeremiah says how long? And that's the question so many people have. How long will it take to be delivered, to be debt free? How long will I be divorced and can't find a life partner? How long will I be alone, broke, busted and disgusted with life? How long will I be distressed, disrespected and depressed? How long before I get myself together? How long before I'm delivered from debt ? How long before I get married, before I become a citizen? Have you ever been in a place, in a situation that has taken longer than expected? (John chapter 5, a man was sick for 38 years. He was not 38 years old, but he was sick for 38 years.)

Luke 13:11 KJV

[11] And, behold, there was a woman which had a spirit of infirmity eighteen years, and was bowed together, and could in no wise lift up herself.

Mark 5:25-26 KJV

[25] And a certain woman, which had an issue of blood twelve years, [26] And had suffered many things of many physicians, and had spent all that she had, and was nothing bettered, but rather grew worse,

38 years, 18 years, and 12 years. How long have you been believing God can turn your situation around? Sometimes our situation lasts longer. Most of us are crying, "How long?"

Isaiah 49:14-16 KJV

[14] But Zion said, The Lord hath forsaken me, and my Lord hath forgotten me. [15] Can a woman forget her sucking child, that she should not have compassion on the son of her womb? yea, they may forget, yet will I not forget thee. [16] Behold, I have graven thee upon the palms of my hands; thy walls are continually before me.

Sometimes we feel God has forsaken us, and we feel rejected. We feel like God has forgotten us.

Hebrews 13:5 KJV

for he hath said, I will never leave thee, nor forsake thee.

Hebrews 6:10 KJV

[10] For God is not unrighteous to forget your work and labour of love, which ye have shewed toward his name, in that ye have ministered to the saints, and do minister.

I have come to encourage you. And I believe with all my heart and with everything inside of me, it won't take that long.

"Yes indeed, it won't be long now." God's Decree. "Things are going to happen so fast your head will swim. One fast thing on the heels of the other. You won't be able to keep up. Everything will be happening at once—and everywhere you look, blessings! Blessings like wine pouring off the mountains and hills. I'll make everything right again for my people Israel."

In John chapter six, there is a great crowd following Jesus. In verse two, they're following him because of the miraculous signs. Show me a sign. It is not enough to confess or profess that you are a child of God.

And there was no miracle, there was no sign. There is no evidence. This is the generation and this is a season. We need to believe and trust God to make an evidence of blessings, an evidence of favor. Evidence of prosperity as a child of God. Make an evidence of fruitfulness.

Isaiah 8:18 KJV

[18] Behold, I and the children whom the Lord hath given me are for signs and for wonders in Israel from the Lord of hosts, which dwelleth in mount Zion.

"Gideon replied, "If now I have found favor in your eyes, give me a sign that it is really you talking to me."

Judges 6:17 NIV

God if you are ready with me, show me a sign. Nothing cancels insults like results. If we don't have signs, and wonders and miracles, people will insult us and insult the God we serve.

Mark 16:17 KJV

[17] And these signs shall follow them that believe; In my name shall they cast out devils; they shall speak with new tongues;

Those of us who believe signs are supposed to follow us.

Jesus sits down after teaching and ministering the word of God to all the people. Jesus sits down with his disciples. You have to learn self care. You have to learn how to take care of yourself. Sometimes we do too much. We are always taking care of other people. We're taking care of children, taking care of your spouse, taking care of mothers, taking care of fathers, taking care of this and that, and sometimes we forget to take care of ourselves. A lot of people are suffering from burnout. When you're on a flight, the air hostess will tell you in case of an emergency to put on your oxygen mask before you try to put on somebody else's. She's telling you to take care of yourself before you try to help somebody else. A lot of us are hurting, but you're trying to help other people.

A lot of us are discouraged. But we are trying to encourage other people. A lot of us are drowning, but we're trying to teach somebody else how to swim. You have to take care of yourself.

Mark 12:31 KJV

[31] And the second is like, namely this, Thou shalt love thy neighbour as thyself. There is none other commandment greater than these.

Jesus said, Love your neighbor as yourself. If you do not love yourself, how can you love your neighbor? This is not being selfish. This is not being arrogant. This is not being proud. This is being wise. It's a blessing to be good and help other people. But you have to make sure you help and take care of yourself. The prodigal son came to his senses. He said, "I will arise. I will go to my father's house." As long as he's feeding pigs, he's not helping himself. He's hungry. He's in the mud. He's working with pigs, which is beneath his spiritual dignity and capacity. He said this is the season that I have to take care of myself. I have to arise. It is said and believed if you want something done right , you have to do it yourself. After ministering and pouring out, Jesus took some time.

Psalm 90:12 KJV

[12] So teach us to number our days, that we may apply our hearts unto wisdom.

You have to set your house in order before you try to set somebody else's house in order.

Matthew 7:5 KJV

[5] Thou hypocrite, first cast out the beam out of thine own eye; and then shalt thou see clearly to cast out the mote out of thy brother's eye.

Learn how to take care of yourself.

Luke 4:23 KJV

[23] And he said unto them, Ye will surely say unto me this proverb, Physician, heal thyself: whatsoever we have heard done in Capernaum, do also here in thy country.

Learn how to believe in yourself,

Shakespeare said : to thine own self be true,

And it must follow, as the night the day, Thou canst not then be false to any man.

Learn how to encourage yourself.

1 Samuel 30:6 KJV

[6] And David was greatly distressed; for the people spake of

stoning him, because the soul of all the people was grieved, every man for his sons and for his daughters: but David encouraged himself in the Lord his God.

In verse five, Jesus looked up and said to Phillip, “Where can we buy bread before the people get here?” He is making preparations.

Jesus is already making preparations for your next blessing. Your next house, your next marriage, your next assignment, scholarship businesses.

Luke 14:17 KJV

[17] And sent his servant at supper time to say to them that were bidden, Come; for all things are now ready.

Psalm 23:5 KJV

[5] Thou preparest a table before me in the presence of mine enemies: thou anointest my head with oil; my cup runneth over.

Romans 8:32 KJV

[32] He that spared not his own Son, but delivered him up for us all, how shall he not with him also freely give us all things?

Jesus is making preparation.

I want you to understand, God never waits until you get in a situation and says, “What would I do?”

Jeremiah 29:11 KJV

[11] For I know the thoughts that I think toward you, saith the Lord, thoughts of peace, and not of evil, to give you an expected end.

God knows the end from the beginning. He already knows your tomorrow before you get in your tomorrow.

He did this to test Philip to see if Philip would think like him. Where can we buy bread? A lot of us have failed the test. When at the enormity of the situation, challenges and problems, we believe what the world is saying more than what God is saying. You have to think like Jesus.

1 Corinthians 2:16 KJV

[16] For who hath known the mind of the Lord, that he may instruct him? But we have the mind of Christ.

Philippians 2:5 KJV

[5] Let this mind be in you, which was also in Christ Jesus

Philip failed the test. He's thinking like the world. We don't have enough money. We are broke. We are busted. We are disgusted. I'm a single parent. I do not have an education. I do not have a degree. I'm not married. I'm not yet a citizen. I'm not a millionaire. When you begin to think like Jesus, all things are possible.

How can I get the house? God will provide. How am I going to get married? God will make a way. How will my children go to college? God is able. You have to think like God.

“Philip answered him, “It would take more than half a year’s wages to buy enough bread for each one to have a bite!” John 6:7 NIV

In verse seven he says eight months salary is not enough. More than half a year’s will not be sufficient

“Another of his disciples, Andrew, Simon Peter’s brother, spoke up, “Here is a boy with five small barley loaves and two small fish, but how far will they go among so many?” John 6:8-9 NIV

“Jesus said, “Have the people sit down.” There was plenty of grass in that place, and they sat down (about five thousand men were there).” John 6:10 NIV

It won't take that long for you to be delivered. For you to be set free, to get the house, get married, get the scholarship, citizenship, for your son to come out of prison, for your husband to be delivered, for your mother to be totally healed. It won’t take that long. What took others years will take you months. What took other months will take you days. What took others days will take you minutes. What took other minutes will take you seconds. It won't take that long.

“Yes indeed, it won’t be long now.” God’s Decree. “Things are going to happen so fast your head will swim, one thing fast on the heels of the other. You won’t be able to keep up. Everything will be happening at once—and everywhere you look, blessings! Blessings

I want you to believe in God. Because you are connected to Jesus, He will supply all Your needs according to His riches and glory (Philippians 4:19)

It won't take that long. I have five loaves and two fish. God is getting ready to connect you with the right people. People of influence. People with resources. People that can underwrite Your dreams, your ideas, your vision.

Proverbs 27:17 KJV

[17] Iron sharpeneth iron; so a man sharpeneth the countenance of his friend.

God connected Joseph with a butler and the baker. The butler remembered him. He came out of prison to interpret dreams and became the Prime Minister.

The disciples knew the problem, but never had the solution. The young boy had the solution, but never knew the problem.

I see God connecting you to the right people.

Moses and Joshua, Naomi and Ruth, Elijah and Elisha, Paul and Timothy, Mary and Elizabeth.

May you never miss those you are supposed to meet, and never meet those you're supposed to miss. Whoever is around you but against you, may they be disconnected from you.

Deuteronomy 22:10 KJV

[10] Thou shalt not plow with an ox and an ass together.

Proverbs 13:20 KJV

[20] He that walketh with wise men shall be wise: but a companion of fools shall be destroyed.

Psalm 1:1 KJV

[1] Blessed is the man that walketh not in the counsel of the ungodly, nor standeth in the way of sinners, nor sitteth in the seat of the scornful.

1 Corinthians 15:33 KJV

[33] Be not deceived: evil communications corrupt good manners.

Five loaves and two fish. Five plus two equals seven. Seven is the number of completion.

It won't take that long. When God blesses you, He completes you

Colossians 2:10 KJV

[10] And ye are complete in him, which is the head of all principality and power:

God will never bless us and leave us incomplete.

5 loaves of bread, more bread than fish. Bread represents Jesus.

John 6:48 KJV

I am the bread of life.

Bread represents the Word of God.

Get your word. Have more word in you. Spend time reading your Bible.

Joshua 1:8 KJV

[8] This book of the law shall not depart out of thy mouth; but thou shalt meditate therein day and night, that thou mayest observe to do according to all that is written therein: for then thou shalt make thy way prosperous, and then thou shalt have good success.

Deuteronomy 28:1-3 KJV

[1] And it shall come to pass, if thou shalt hearken diligently unto the voice of the Lord thy God, to observe and to do all his commandments which I command thee this day, that the Lord thy God will set thee on high above all nations of the earth: [2] And all these blessings shall come on thee, and overtake thee, if thou shalt hearken unto the voice of the Lord thy God. [3] Blessed shalt thou be in the city, and blessed shalt thou be in the field.

Invest more time in the Word of God. It won't be long now. It won't take that long.

Fish represent signs and miracles. When you get hold of the Word of God, miracles will follow.

Jesus said have the people sit down and all of them ate and they were satisfied. Your blessing won't take that long. Your promotion won't take that long. Your healing won't take that long. I want you to believe God. They were satisfied. Bread of heaven Feed me till I want no more. Feast on the Word of God. It won't take that long.

I DEMAND AN APPOINTMENT (MARK 10:46-50)

Let me start by saying don't wait. Don't schedule, and don't beg for an appointment. Demand your appointment.

Matthew 11:12 KJV

[12] And from the days of John the Baptist until now the kingdom of heaven suffereth violence, and the violent take it by force.

"When you are gentle, you don't settle. You end up in a ghetto. You never get to your God given destination."

Gentility is an error in the place of warfare.

1 Chronicles 12:32 KJV

[32] And of the children of Issachar, which were men that had understanding of the times, to know what Israel ought to do; the heads of them were two hundred; and all their brethren were at their commandment.

You must understand this is the time and season for an appointment with God that will change your situation, condition and challenges of your life forever. We're introduced to a character named Bartimaeus. His biological father's name is Timaeus. Bartimaeus is blind and there are a couple of things about Bartimaeus I want you to see.

There are so many disadvantages in his life. But he never complained. He never begged God to die, he never ate carpet dust. He never felt sorry for himself. He knew his time would come.

Psalm 102:13 KJV

[13] Thou shalt arise, and have mercy upon Zion: for the time to favour her, yea, the set time, is come.

The first thing I see is that he's at a place called Jericho. Jericho is a cursed place.

Joshua 6:26 KJV

[26] And Joshua adjured them at that time, saying, Cursed be the man before the Lord, that riseth up and buildeth this city Jericho: he shall lay the foundation thereof in his firstborn, and in his youngest son shall he set up the gates of it.

When you are at a cursed place or are dealing with curses, your family is cursed, dealing with generational curses. Or you look at your life and family and realize nobody in your family has ever made it. You can’t seem to get ahead. You take two steps forward and 10 steps backwards. You are always behind in life, and feel like you are under a curse. You are working, but broke. Praying with no answers. Fasting with no deliverance. Your children are not doing well. Marriage is on the rocks, and can never settle. You are the tail instead of being the head, though you have the skills and the intelligence to be successful in life. You always find yourself at the bottom. You are at the valley instead of being at the mountain top. Good things always manage to slip through your fingers. Barrenness and unfruitfulness is present.

When your life is meeting the evil expectations of your enemies.

Joblessness, particularly in the midst of plenty.

You are beautiful, old enough and desire to marry but cannot. You've never been approached for marriage. In some cases, you are always in the wrong relationship. You are constantly rejected and disappointed in all areas of your life.

Pattern of rising and falling.

Famine and lack of any sort.

Hardship - always finding it hard to make a breakthrough.

When a person is under a curse not only does it bring shame and disgrace, it brings sadness, weeping and tears. It brings sorrow and a broken heart.

If this has been your life you need to cry out to God to break the curse from your life and family.

He's at a cursed place.

Jericho also represents the wall . It stands for division. One of the greatest weapons of the enemy is division.

If the enemy can divide us, he can destroy us.

Mark 3:25 KJV

[25] And if a house be divided against itself, that house cannot stand.

Romans 16:17 KJV

[17] Now I beseech you, brethren, mark them which cause divisions and offences contrary to the doctrine which ye have learned; and avoid them.

You have to deal with the spirit of division. Many marriages are divided. Husbands and wives living in separate rooms. Siblings are divided, churches are divided, pastors are divided, church members are divided. Pastors don't speak to each other. The enemy hates unity. You have to deal with the spirit of division. You have to declare my house, my marriage, my family, my ministry will not be divided.

Jericho is a place of warfare. You know you are at Jericho because you're dealing with unnecessary battles. Every day you have to fight. You are in the fight of your life. Every day is an argument. Every day you are dealing with something negative in your life, on your job, with your family, with your spouse, with your children, etc.

You can never experience peace for a day. You are under so

much pressure and you can never experience pleasure. You're always tense, always angered. Always crawling and scratching when nothing is itching. Dealing with unnecessary battles from family members, co-workers. One of the reasons David could not build the temple for God was because of too many battles, too much blood on his hands. One of the reasons a lot of people cannot accomplish and cannot be fulfilled is because they are dealing with too many unnecessary battles.

The second thing is to realize He's sitting. He's at one place. He's dealing with stagnation. As long as the enemy can stagnant you, he can limit you and eventually destroy you.

Exodus 14:13 KJV

[13] And Moses said unto the people, Fear ye not, stand still, and see the salvation of the Lord, which he will shew to you to day: for the Egyptians whom ye have seen to day, ye shall see them again no more for ever.

Moses told the children of Israel to stand still but God said no, I know you are a prophet but you miss it , in verse 15 that spoke to Moses

Exodus 14:15 KJV

[15] And the Lord said unto Moses, Wherefore criest thou unto me? speak unto the children of Israel, that they go forward:

I pray whatever has stagnated your life be broken from your life today in Jesus Mighty Name.

Acts 17:28 KJV

[28] For in him we live, and move, and have our being; as certain also of your own poets have said, For we are also his offspring.

The next thing is he's by the road side. He's not on the way, he's not on the road. He's by the roadside. Jesus is the way and he wants you to be in the way. Any time you are by the way and not in the way, you are not in His will. You are not in His purpose. The enemy gets excited. The enemy wants you to be by the way, spiritually by the way, financially by the way.

In your marriage, you are not happy. You are a wife, but you are not the focus of attention and attraction. Another woman is. You are a mother by the way, You are a sister by the way. Your business is by the way. It simply means you are not progressing. You are not making headway.

He is not established because he's by the roadside. He has to wait for people to give to him so he's dealing with the spirit of dependability.

You have to depend on Social Security. You have to depend on the government. You have to depend on child support. You have to depend on unemployment. You have to depend on a man. As long as you live in the life of dependability, you are living a life of limitation, restriction and frustration. Dependability will incapacitate your life, your destiny and future. That's not God's will for you.

Psalm 34:5 KJV

[5] They looked unto him, and were lightened: and their faces were not ashamed.

Psalm 121:1 KJV

[1] I will lift up mine eyes unto the hills, from whence cometh my help.

Psalm 20:7 KJV

[7] Some trust in chariots, and some in horses: but we will remember the name of the Lord our God.

Jeremiah 17:5 KJV

[5] Thus saith the Lord ; Cursed be the man that trusteth in man, and maketh flesh his arm, and whose heart departeth from the Lord.

I pray your dependability will never be in a man, government, or a system. Your dependability will be in God and God alone

He's blind, No vision

Helen Keller was blind. And a reporter once asked her, What's worse than being blind? She said, having sight without a vision.

Proverbs 29:18 KJV

[18] Where there is no vision, the people perish: but he that keepeth the law, happy is he.

Habakkuk 2:2-3 KJV

[2] And the Lord answered me, and said, Write the vision, and make it plain upon tables, that he may run that readeth it. [3] For the vision is yet for an appointed time, but at the end it shall speak, and not lie: though it tarry, wait for it; because it will surely come, it will not tarry.

Jeremiah 1:11-12 KJV

[11] Moreover the word of the Lord came unto me, saying, Jeremiah, what seest thou? And I said, I see a rod of an almond tree. [12] Then said the Lord unto me, Thou hast well seen: for I will hasten my word to perform it.

Vision is the ability to see ahead. Vision is the ability to see your tomorrow today. Vision gives you direction. Vision simplifies your life. If you don't have a vision you will never go far. If you don't have a vision of where you're going, any exit will take you, or you will take an exit along the way. When you don't have a vision you eat anything, you go anywhere. But if you have a vision you spend your time wisely. You spend your money wisely. You have time to go to bed. There are certain friends you don't keep. When You have vision, you don't waste time around foolishness. You're very focused. Very intentional. Very purposeful.

He's blind and cannot see. Where there is no vision you will Perish.

He's a beggar.

Psalm 37:25 KJV

[25] I have been young, and now am old; yet have I not seen the righteous forsaken, nor his seed begging bread.

I've been around and I've seen the London Bridge. I've seen Piccadilly circle. I've seen Big Ben. I have seen the Brooklyn Bridge. I've seen the Statue of Liberty. I've seen the White House. I've seen the blue waters of the Bahamas. I've seen the Kwame Nkrumah circle. I've seen Jamaica. I've seen some of the finest bank and cheese in Switzerland.

One thing I have not seen: I have not seen the righteous forsaken. I have not seen God's people beg for bread. He's a beggar. May the spirit of begging never be your portion. May God bring you into the spirit of plenty, spirit of wealth, and the spirit of overflow.

Something changed in his life. He heard the old mothers sing, Jesus is passing this way, this way, this way..........

Romans 10:17 KJV

[17] So then faith cometh by hearing, and hearing by the word of God.

John 10:27 KJV

[27] My sheep hear my voice, and I know them, and they follow me:

Ruth 1:6 KJV

[6] Then she arose with her daughters in law, that she might return from the country of Moab: for she had heard in the country of Moab how that the Lord had visited his people in giving them bread.

Naomi heard that God had visited his people. What are you hearing? Elijah heard the sound of abundance. What you hear, determines where you go and what you receive. I hear abundance for you. I hear overflow. I hear scholarship. I hear citizenship. I hear a meaningful relationship. I hear blessing. I hear increase. You know what I don't hear. I don't hear poverty. I don't hear demonic activity. I do not hear lack. I do not hear insufficiency. I do not hear divorce. I do not hear incarceration. I do not hear miscarriage. I hear abundance. He heard. What are you hearing? And he shouted. This is not the time to be quiet. You must open your mouth.

Psalm 81:10 KJV

[10] I am the Lord thy God, which brought thee out of the land of Egypt: open thy mouth wide, and I will fill it.

Open mouth, open Heaven. Closed mouth, closed Heaven. The strength of the oppressor is the silence of the oppressed. Whatever is oppressing an individual's life will continue to oppress them as long as they are silent.

Job 13:19 KJV

[19] Who is he that will plead with me? for now, if I hold my tongue, I shall give up the ghost.

You have to learn to open your mouth. You have to learn to cry out to God

Psalm 55:17-18 KJV

[17] Evening, and morning, and at noon, will I pray, and cry aloud: and he shall hear my voice. [18] He hath delivered my soul in peace from the battle that was against me: for there were many with me.

Psalm 61:1-2 KJV

[1] Hear my cry, O God; attend unto my prayer. [2] From the end of the earth will I cry unto thee, when my heart is overwhelmed: lead me to the rock that is higher than I.

He began to shout. He demanded an appointment with Jesus. He said I have to meet you in person. And the Bible says they rebuked him, they told him to be quiet, to shut up. A lot of people don't mind you begging, struggling asking them for help. As long as you're on the same level, as long as you are broke, not married, have a dead end job. Limited and restricted, confused and abused. They don't mind. But as soon as you start shouting for change, they have a problem.

As soon as you make up your mind to go back to school, to get married, to get a better job, to move from an apartment, to a house, to be debt free, they have a problem. As long as he's on the same level, stagnated, not moving and begging, they never rebuke him. It is my prayer that your haters will become your elevators. Some people will tell you it doesn't take all that, you don't have to shout. You don't have to pray. You don't have to do all that running, dancing, and giving. But I pray God uses your enemies to inspire you. Because this time around, he's not begging for money. He's not begging for a ride. He's not begging for a handout. He's shouting for change. He's shouting to have an appointment with Jesus. He's shouting because he needs a miracle. He's shouting because he needs a favor from the master. He needs his eyes to be opened. He needs his life to be restored. You have to shout for change. You have to shout for a blessing and a miracle. You have to shout for your family to be delivered.

You have to shout until your situation changes, until immigration is approved, your paperwork is approved. You cannot allow people to stop you from shouting for a change.

He's crying for change and they start hating because people want you to be quiet and depressed, quiet and struggling, quiet and broke, busted and disgusted. Quiet and in pain. But you have to learn how to shout.

He said Son of David, have mercy on me. He's a student of the Bible, and knows the genealogy of Jesus. He said have mercy. God is a merciful God. He said I will have mercy on Zion. He said in his wrath he will remember mercy. You can tell Bartimaeus is a praiser and he shouts until Jesus stops. He said I won't stop until I get an appointment.

Isaiah 58:1 KJV

[1] Cry aloud, spare not, lift up thy voice like a trumpet, and shew my people their transgression, and the house of Jacob their sins.

Jesus stopped, Jesus called him. There's a call of God on your life. A call for greatness. A call to become all he intends you to be. A call to rise from where you've been to where you need to be. A call to break the curse in your family and in your generation. A calltTo make an impact in your world. A call to put your doubters to shame. A call to damage the devil.

Jesus called him and he jumped to his feet. He cheered up. He threw away his clock.

Mark 10:50 KJV

[50] And he, casting away his garment, rose, and came to Jesus.

He said, I refuse to wear the garment of blindness, the garment of poverty, the garment of being a beggar. The garment of stagnation, the garment of limitation. You have to throw away limitations. You got to throw away restrictions. You have to throw away stagnation. You have to declare, I will not wear the garment of poverty. I have a call on my life. I refuse to wear the garment of demonic attack.

Jesus asked him, What do you want me to do for you? And the problem that I have with this blind man, he's been blind for so long.

His condition has limited his ability and excellence. This blind man only asked for one thing. When you get in the presence of God, you can't just ask for one thing. He should have asked for his life to be restored for all the years that have been wasted. He should have asked for Jesus to establish him, bless his family. Sometimes when you deal with a situation all of your life, it takes your confidence, your excellence and your drive.

Romans 8:32 KJV

[32] He that spared not his own Son, but delivered him up for us all, how shall he not with him also freely give us all things?

2 Corinthians 9:8 KJV

[8] And God is able to make all grace abound toward you; that ye, always having all sufficiency in all things, may abound to every good work:

God wants to give you all things, but he wants you to ask and it shall be given to you.

This is where the enemy made the mistake. The enemy took his sight. But the enemy should have taken his voice. As long as you have your voice, you can demand an appointment, a change, a blessing, a miracle and a breakingthrough

Numbers 14:28 KJV

[28] Say unto them, As truly as I live, saith the Lord, as ye have spoken in mine ears, so will I do to you:

Job 22:28 KJV

[28] Thou shalt also decree a thing, and it shall be established unto thee: and the light shall shine upon thy ways.

Psalm 107:2 KJV

[2] Let the redeemed of the Lord say so, whom he hath redeemed from the hand of the enemy;

Mark 11:23 KJV

[23] For verily I say unto you, That whosoever shall say unto this mountain, Be thou removed, and be thou cast into the sea; and shall not doubt in his heart, but shall believe that those things which he saith shall come to pass; he shall have whatsoever he saith.

Remember, if you remain silent, nothing will happen. But if you want change, shout and praise God until you see something.

What do you want? He should have said, I want to see. I want a house. I want a car, I want a wife. I want a successful career, etc.

Jesus said go your faith hath made thee whole and immediately he received a sight.

Follow Jesus in the way not by the way.

I pray you will not just get an appointment with Bill Gates ,

Barack Obama, with Jeff Bezos and Oprah Winfrey. I pray you get an appointment with the King of kings and Lord of lords.

JUST DO IT

In John chapter two, Jesus is invited to a wedding. It's a celebration. He was invited to a wedding where two people were coming together. Before you do anything in life, invite Jesus to show up. Invite Jesus in your marriage. Invite Jesus in your home. Invite Jesus in your ministry. Invite Jesus in your business.

Invite Jesus in your decision making. Invite Jesus in raising your children. Invite Jesus.

Proverbs 3:6 KJV

[6] In all thy ways acknowledge him, and he shall direct thy paths

Matthew 6:33 KJV

[33] But seek ye first the kingdom of God, and his righteousness; and all these things shall be added unto you.

Before they did anything they invited Jesus. Do you notice they never invited the devil and never invited demons? They never invited depression, witchcraft, or satanic spirits. You have to speak and declare, "Devil, you are not invited in my home, in my marriage, in my children's life, in my finances, my dream, my vision, and in my assignment."

They invited Jesus and they ran out of wine. When they ran out of wine, Mary goes to Jesus saying, “They have no more wine.”

Please do not make God your last option, make him your first option. When things are going good and things are going wel a lot of people do not call on Jesus. The only time we call AAA is when our car breaks down. God is not the CEO of AAA or roadside assistance.

God is not your pimp. God is not your sugar daddy. Our relationship with God cannot be with God only for God to take care of our problems and troubles of life. We call him when we want him to supply, provide, and make a way. That cannot be the only time we call on to him.

Psalm 42:1-2 KJV

[1] As the heart panteth after the water brooks, so panteth my soul after thee, O God. [2] My soul thirsteth for God, for the living God: when shall I come and appear before God?

Psalm 63:1-2 KJV

[1] O God, thou art my God; early will I seek thee: my soul thirsteth for thee, my flesh longeth for thee in a dry and thirsty land, where no water is; [2] To see thy power and thy glory, so as I have seen thee in the sanctuary.

Don’t make Jesus your last option.

On the third day they ran out of wine. Mary the mother of Jesus goes to Jesus and begins to plead and intercede on their behalf.

God is looking for intercessors. God is looking for people that can pray and intercede on behalf of another. Sometimes, we are so caught up in ourselves we forget about other people.

John 15:13 KJV

[13] Greater love hath no man than this, that a man lay down his life for his friends.

Ezekiel 22:30 KJV

[30] And I sought for a man among them, that should make up the hedge, and stand in the gap before me for the land, that I should not destroy it: but I found none.

I'm praying that God will deliver us from selfishness. Me, myself and I. My name is Jimmy, what can you give me? It's all about us. But I'm trusting God to raise up people that want to see other people blessed, other people healed, delivered and set free. See other people get married. Other people fulfilled their God given destiny.

Mary begins to intercede on behalf of this family and she tells the servants whatever he tells them to do, just do it. Jesus said, “Don't get me involved. My time has not come.” But because of Mary’s relationship with Jesus, she knows his capability. She knows the anointing on his Life. God is going to deliver somebody because of your relationship with Him. God is going to heal somebody because of your relationship with Him. God is going to save families. God will set people free because of your relationship with Him.

Whatever he tells you to do, just do it. Don’t argue, don't rationalize, don't analyze from a logical philosophical theological and scientific point of view. Just do it. Obedience is better than Sacrifice. (1 Sam 15:22)

Isaiah 1:19 KJV

[19] If ye be willing and obedient, ye shall eat the good of the land:

Job 36:11 KJV

[11] If they obey and serve him, they shall spend their days in prosperity, and their years in pleasures.

When you obey God, He shows up and shows out. The blessings of the Lord will catch you.

Turn nothing into something.Hopelessness into hope. Questions into answers. Tests into testimonies. Failure into success. Obstacles into miracles. Shame into glory. Just do it. He said, fill the pot with water.

Ephesians 5:26 KJV

[26] That he might sanctify and cleanse it with the washing of water by the word,

Fill the vessel with water. Fill your life with the water of the word. Allow the Spirit of God to fill your home. Fill your marriage. Fill your children. Fill your business with the Word of God.

Jesus is the answer. Stop filling your life with junk. Stop filling your life with garbage. He said fill the pot with water. The pot is a vessel representing your life. Water is a type of the word and the spirit. Fill your life with God's word.

Colossians 3:16 KJV

[16] Let the word of Christ dwell in you richly in all wisdom; teaching and admonishing one another in psalms and hymns and spiritual songs, singing with grace in your hearts to the Lord.

He filled them to the brim and Jesus turned the Water into wine.

Luke 21:13 KJV

[13] And it shall turn to you for a testimony.

Psalm 126:1 KJV

[1] When the Lord turned again the captivity of Zion, we were like them that dream.

God is turning it around for your testimony. He's gonna turn your family around, turn your child around, turn your marriage around, turn your money around.

He told them to take it to the master of the banquet, take it to the governor of the banquet.

When he tasted the water that was turned into wine, he called the bridegroom and said, everyone brings the choice wine first then the cheaper wine. But you have saved the best for last.

Untill now you've been through some things in your life. Some discouragement, some heart break, abuse, molestation, divorce, separation, termination, sicknesses, illnesses. But you are saved for the best. God said the reason why you did not die is because I saved you for the best. The best marriage, the best career, the best house, the best school, the best wife, the best husband, the best health. The best position, the best clothes, the best. I saved you for the best.

I didn't save you for what is cheap. I did not save you to be tolerated. I saved you for the best.

Do not settle for less, but settle for the best

Everyone brings the choice. Everyone brings what is cheap. But God said I saved you for the best. The wine never ran out again. You will never run out of peace. You will never run out of money. You will never run out of joy. You will never run out of prosperity. You will never run out of happiness. You will never run out of integrity. You will never run out because you are saved for the best.

1 Peter 2:9 KJV

[9] But ye are a chosen generation, a royal priesthood, an holy nation, a peculiar people; that ye should shew forth the praises of him who hath called you out of darkness into his marvellous light:

Marvin Sapp sang a song, "You saw the best in me." When all others could only see all the worst. God saw the best. Others saw failure, disappointment and nothing. They said you would never amount to anything other than a loser, a divorcee. But God saw the best. And I want you to understand, you are saved for the best, by the best. God bless

Stop cutting yourself

Mark 5:1-20

Jesus has just come out of a storm in (Mark 4). A man shows up living in tombs, living with people that are dead. How do you function when you are connected to people who have dead dreams, dead vision, and their ambition, their goals, prayer life, and relationship with God are dead?

He's connected to people that are alive. He is connected to dreamers, praisers, to inventors, to visionaries, or to worshipers. You must refuse to connect with dead people.

Romans 12:1 KJV

[1] I beseech you therefore, brethren, by the mercies of God, that ye present your bodies a living sacrifice, holy, acceptable unto God, which is your reasonable service.

Moreover, he's dealing with people that came to tie him down. Be very careful with people that want to tie you down, want to limit you, suppress you, stagnate your progress, keep you in one spot. They tie his hands and feet. Hands represent blessing, prosperity and productivity. Be very careful with people that want to see you bound.

They don't want to see you prosper. Don't want to see you productive in life. In your marriage, in your ministry, in your career. They tie his hands. God will send you people that will not tie your hands, but People that will celebrate you and the blessing of the Lord over your life. People that will add to you and not take from you

Proverbs 10:22 KJV

[22] The blessing of the Lord, it maketh rich, and he addeth no sorrow with it.

They tied his feet, feet representing movement, acceleration and progress. Be very careful with people that do not want you to progress and do not want you to accelerate. Do not want you to move, but want to see you in the same spot in the same location in the same position.

What is so interesting, he is so strong, he breaks free from the chain. They tie him up, but he could break free from dead people. He could not stop cutting himself.

Zechariah 4:6 KJV

[6] Then he answered and spake unto me, saying, This is the word of the Lord unto Zerubbabel, saying, Not by might, nor by power, but by my spirit, saith the Lord of hosts.

A lot of times we're unable to break free from certain things, certain limitations and restrictions.

But there are things we need the Spirit of God for. We need the help of God. How can you break free from chains holding your legs and your feet, but you cannot break free from dead relationships, dead dreams, dead visions?

He also could not break free from cutting himself. Are you able to break free from speaking negative words? Break free from cursing, break free from being addicted to Facebook and social media? Break free From limiting yourself?

He could break free from what other people put on him, but he could not break free from deadness around him. The Bible says he's crying and cutting himself. Stop cutting yourself. Today we blame the devil. We blame the witch in the village. We blame our ex. We blame our supervisors. We blame the President. We blame everybody else. But we need to stop cutting ourselves. The greatest problem is not the devil. The greatest problem is you.

I hear people say people are looking down on me. People can not look down on you unless you are down. Nobody can make you feel inferior without your permission, you can never change what you accept.

Numbers 13:33 KJV

[33] And there we saw the giants, the sons of Anak, which come of the giants: and we were in our own sight as grasshoppers, and so we were in their sight.

David had to encourage himself. The prodigal son came to himself. You cannot confess negativity over your life and expect other people to speak positively over your life. You cannot hate yourself and expect other people to love you.

Stop cutting yourself.

I met a young lady that went through divorce and she said, "I will never get married again. I will never love a man again. I will never trust a man." That is a self imposed curse.

Proverbs 6:2 KJV

[2] Thou art snared with the words of thy mouth, thou art taken with the words of thy mouth.

She's cutting herself. A lot of people want to be happy in marriage, and want to be happy in life, but they are not doing things to make them happy.

Matthew 12:33 KJV

[33] Either make the tree good, and his fruit good; or else make the tree corrupt, and his fruit corrupt: for the tree is known by his fruit.

The key is in your hand, You can make your life good or you can make your life corrupt. Not the devil. Not God. Not your pastor. Not your spouse. Not your parents. You.

He is cutting himself.

Stop cutting yourself. Stop limiting yourself, stop looking down on yourself. Stop being inferior. Stop having low self esteem. Nobody can help him because he's hurting himself. As long as you are cutting yourself, hurting yourself, nobody can help you. The therapist cannot help you. The preacher cannot help you. Medication cannot help you, counseling can not help you. You have to learn how to help yourself. You have to learn how to encourage yourself. You got to learn how to speak over your life. Speak over your destiny. You have to tell yourself, I can do it. I'm an overcomer. I'm more than a conqueror.

Shakespeare said “to thine own self be true”

Jesus got out of the boat and the man with the evil spirit ran to Jesus. He ran away from dead people. You have to run away from dead people. Dead churches, dead preachers, dead friends, dead relationships, dead job, dead career. You got to run like Joseph.

“She caught him by his cloak and said, “Come to bed with me!” But he left his cloak in her hand and ran out of the house.”

Genesis 39:12 NIV

He ran to Jesus. When he's hurt, when he's broken, when he's wounded, he starts worshiping. It's easy to worship God, it's easy to pray, it's easy to praise, it's easy to give, to love God when everything is alright.

But can you worship when you are hurting? Can you worship when a man walks out of your life?

Can you worship when you get fired? Can you worship when you got more bills than money? Can you worship when people you help hurt you? Can you worship when people turn their backs on you? Can you worship when you get a negative report from the doctor?

Can you worship when your father disowns you and was never around? Can you worship when your son is incarcerated and your daughter leaves the house? Can you still worship while you are broken, while you are hurting, whilst you are wounded? God is looking for wounded worshipers. God is looking for people that are not perfect but can still worship. You know about my issues, you know about my problem, but can you understand my worship?

And the demons begin to cry out. The evil spirit in this man begin to cry now. What do you want with us? And Jesus said, come out of this man, you evil spirit. Everything in us that is not of God is coming out. Bitterness, pain, pride, depression, rejection, loneliness, insecurities, low self esteem and fear are coming out.

And this man was set free and he was delivered because Jesus spoke the word.

Psalm 107:20 KJV

[20] He sent his word, and healed them, and delivered them from their destruction.

After today you will not cut yourself. You will not cry yourself to sleep. You will not eat carpet dust. You will not be overlooked. You will not beg God to die. You will rise above the challenges, disappointments, and difficulties of life.

Jesus spoke to this man and said go home to your family. So how much the Lord Has done for you? How has He had mercy on you? The same applies to you today. Stop cutting yourself. Your family is depending on you. Your generation depends on you. Your community is depending on you. Your children are depending on you. Stop cutting yourself

Talk to the Hand

(Matthew 12:9-13)

Jesus walked in church and saw a man with a withered hand.

His hand is withering, but he's still worshiping. He's still in church.

The word wither means dry, not growing, to lose vitality and freshness.

He's withering but still worshiping. You know you are a true worshiper when things are withering -- marriage, finances, ideas, your dreams, vision, and family -- but you are still worshiping. He's in church not the club, liquor store, Las Vegas casino, or at happy hour.

Psalm 84:7 KJV

[7] They go from strength to strength, every one of them in Zion appeareth before God.

Psalm 84:10 KJV

[10] For a day in thy courts is better than a thousand. I had rather be a doorkeeper in the house of my God, than to dwell in the tents of wickedness.

Psalm 23:6 KJV

[6] Surely goodness and mercy shall follow me all the days of my life: and I will dwell in the house of the Lord for ever.

Psalm 27:4 KJV

[4] One thing have I desired of the Lord, that will I seek after; that I may dwell in the house of the Lord all the days of my life, to behold the beauty of the Lord, and to enquire in his temple.

We find the Pharisees and church leaders In church But they are not worshiping They are looking to see if Jesus Will he You this man.

We should come to church to worship, pray and have an encounter with God. While others come to watch, play gossip, be on social media looking at pictures, taking selfies and looking to see who's wearing what, while worship is going on. When you lose your tenacity, your passion and reverence for the house of God, your service and worship becomes casual and the house of God becomes a social gathering and you lose the essence and purpose for coming to the house of God. So your being in church is not to have an encounter with God, but to satisfy your religious conscience and senses.

This man with the withered hand is in church. We do not know his name. We do not know if he was born with the withered hand or if he was in an accident.

But we thank God he's in church. And he still has one good hand, unlike so many people that hide their issues, their challenges and their weaknesses. Everybody knows he has a withered hand. There are a lot of people not delivered because they are discrete. They know how to hide their issues more than others. And a lot of times, church people are very hypocritical. You are pointing fingers, judging and looking down on a person because they had a baby out of wedlock, but you had an abortion. You have learned to hide your issues better than others.

Proverbs 28:13 KJV

[13] He that covereth his sins shall not prosper: but whoso confesseth and forsaketh them shall have mercy.

Psalm 66:18 KJV

[18] If I regard iniquity in my heart, the Lord will not hear me :

The hand is the part of the body that has the ability to hold on and also has the ability to let go. Hands represent blessing, prosperity and productivity. The right hand in the Bible represents power, strength, and authority.

Your hands have the ability to hold on. Hold on to God, hold on to your faith. Hold on to your belief. Hold on to your dreams. Hold on to the profession of your confession. Hold on and never give up.

The hands also have the ability to let go. You have to let stuff go. Let hurt disappointment, pain, stress, bitterness, rejection, dejection, animosity, unforgiveness, low self esteem, regret etc. Let it go.

In verse 13, Jesus begins to talk to the hand. You have to learn how to talk to your hands. Look at your hands and begin to talk to your hand. Whatever you touch will be blessed. You will handle millions of dollars. You will open the door to your new house, your new car. You will lay your hands on the sick and they will recover. You will sign a million dollar check. You will write checks to pay off other people's mortgages, and student loans. You hold on to God and never let go, you have to learn how to talk to your hand.

Deuteronomy 28:12-13 KJV

[12] The Lord shall open unto thee his good treasure, the heaven to give the rain unto thy land in his season, and to bless all the work of thine hand: and thou shalt lend unto many nations, and thou shalt not borrow.

Declare your hands will lend and not borrow. Talk to your hands that from today I will be a lender and not a borrower. I will be an investor and not a waster

"And I will make the Egyptians favorably disposed toward this people, so that when you leave you will not go empty-handed."

Exodus 3:21 NIV

My hand will not be empty. By favor, I talked to my hand. God, put it in my hand. The keys to the house, the car, put my real estate license in my hands. Daycare license, my business license, scholarship, marriage, grant money, promotion, pre approval letter. Opportunity. Put it in my hand. I declare in the next 3 hours, 72 hours, 13 days it will enter my hand. You got to talk to your hands.

Matthew 18:19 KJV

[19] Again I say unto you, That if two of you shall agree on earth as touching any thing that they shall ask, it shall be done for them of my Father which is in heaven.

Whoever you're connected to, that has faith, touch them and come in agreement. As a touch your hands, my daughter is restored. My son is delivered. My husband is saved . My wife is healed. My money is restored. My business is prospering. Touch and talk to your hand.

Psalm 24:3-4 KJV

[3] Who shall ascend into the hill of the Lord ? or who shall stand in his holy place? [4] He that hath clean hands, and a pure heart; who hath not lifted up his soul unto vanity, nor sworn deceitfully.

My hands are clean. They will never do dirt. They will never beat my children. My hands will never strike my wife. My hands will never send nasty text messages. Unbutton, the shirt or blouse of somebody I'm not married to, or unzip somebody's pants, or bring somebody's skirt down that is not a wife or husband. My hands will never go on a porn site. I will never give the middle finger because of road rage.

My hand will not be in anything illegal. My hand will never steal from God or take that which doesn't belong to me. You have to learn how to talk to your hand.

Jesus used his hands to write when the woman was called in adultery. Why? Because he wanted to leave his DNA.

When a criminal is caught they take them for a fingerprint. God wants to clean your hand and fingerprint. So that anything you touch will be blessed.

Jesus said to him stretch out your hand. You have to stretch your hand to your bank account and declare I will never be broke. My account will never be in red. Stretch your hands to your children while they sleep and declare they will never be molested. They will never be on behavior modification drugs, they will never be incarcerated. Stretch your hands to your business and say you will be a fortune 500 company. Stretch your hands to your job and declare God will bless you. God will favor you. Stretch your hands and declare God will increase your income bracket, the square footage of your house. Stretch your hands and declare to your mailbox, there will be no junk mail, but money will be in your mailbox. Letters of approval, contracts, opportunities, and packages of acceleration will be in your mailbox. You have to learn how to talk to your hand.

When he stretched out his hand it was completely restored.

Joel 2:25 KJV

[25] And I will restore to you the years that the locust hath eaten, the cankerworm, and the caterpiller, and the palmerworm, my great army which I sent among you.

Everything that is withering, everything that is dying, everything that is losing vitality, everything that is losing freshness, God is bringing to complete restoration.

You have to learn how to talk to your hand.

THIS WILL NOT TAKE YOU UNDER

Jesus had been teaching all day. He told His disciples, "Let's go over to the other side." Whenever you have learned your lesson, God will not allow you to stagnate. He will shift you to another place, to another dimension, and to higher heights. If you are stuck, and you are stagnate, it simply means you haven't learned yet. So Jesus said, "Let's go over." Not let *me*, but let *us*. When you have learned what God has taught you, and you are anointed, you don't just take yourself. You take your friends, your family, your co-workers, and everybody connected to you, to another dimension.

I can tell you have not learned what God has been teaching you. I can tell you are not truly anointed. Because you only bring yourself in the presence of God. You bring yourself to church. What God has taught you, you must use to affect the lives of others.

The disciples never argued with Jesus or asked why or where they were going.

They were obedient.

Deuteronomy 28:1-3 KJV

[1] And it shall come to pass, if thou shalt hearken diligently unto the voice of the Lord thy God, to observe and to do all his commandments which I command thee this day, that the Lord thy God will set thee on high above all nations of the earth: [2] And all these blessings shall come on thee, and overtake thee, if thou shalt hearken unto the voice of the Lord thy God. [3] Blessed shalt thou be in the city, and blessed shalt thou be in the field.

Job 36:11 KJV

[11] If they obey and serve him, they shall spend their days in prosperity, and their years in pleasures.

Isaiah 1:19 KJV

[19] If ye be willing and obedient, ye shall eat the good of the land:

We have to be obedient.

1 Samuel 15:22 KJV

[22] And Samuel said, Hath the Lord as great delight in burnt offerings and sacrifices, as in obeying the voice of the Lord ? Behold, to obey is better than sacrifice, and to hearken than the fat of rams.

The disciples were obedient. When you are obedient to the call of God, you experience the blessing of the Lord. As the disciples got in the boat, on the way to the other side a strong wind broke out. What happens when you are obedient to the call of God? You are obedient to the voice of God. You are obedient to the instruction God has given you and a storm breaks out in your life. What happens when you obey the voice of God and you are still going through attacks? You are still going through challenges. What happens when you say yes to God and everything is against you.

A lot of times, people think when they say yes to God, or they are obedient to God, they will not go through obstacles, challenges and problems.

2 Timothy 2:12 KJV

[12] If we suffer, we shall also reign with him : if we deny him, he also will deny us:

Psalm 34:19 KJV

[19] Many are the afflictions of the righteous: but the Lord delivereth him out of them all.

It is the part of the gospel we don't like to hear and we don't like to preach.

God's people will suffer every time. You will go through challenges. You will go through hell. You will go through storms. They said yes and they obeyed the call and the voice of God. And a storm broke out. You are in a storm right now. You are going through challenges right now. Don't give up. Don't lose heart. Don't turn your back. There is a bright side. You will get to your God-given destination. Jesus is with them. And they are still going through a storm. Have you ever been there? You are faithful. You are always in the presence of God, worshiping, tithing and yet still, you are going through a storm. And what is interesting is that Jesus is asleep in the storm.

How can you be asleep in my storm? I need you to be up. I've watched you blessed strangers.

I've watched you heal people that were not even following you. People that are not praying. People that are not tithing . People that don't go to church. People that sleep around, don't give and drink alcohol. I've watched you bless them. And I'm a disciple. I'm serving you. I'm with you. And you are asleep in my storm.

Sometimes we question God, and rightfully so. Why? God is not upset. God is not intimidated by you questioning him.

Like the disciples, wake Jesus up and say, "You cannot be sleeping in my storm."

Isaiah 62:7 KJV

[7] And give him no rest, till he establish, and till he make Jerusalem a praise in the earth.

2 Chronicles 7:14 KJV

[14] If my people, which are called by my name, shall humble themselves, and pray, and seek my face, and turn from their

wicked ways; then will I hear from heaven, and will forgive their sin, and will heal their land.

Psalm 55:17-18 KJV

[17] Evening, and morning, and at noon, will I pray, and cry aloud: and he shall hear my voice. [18] He hath delivered my soul in peace from the battle that was against me: for there were many with me.

You've got to wake him up in your storm. You've got to lift up your voice and cry unto him. The storm was trying to drown them. The storm was trying to stop them from getting to the other side. The storm was trying to cause them to doubt the authenticity of the Word of God. Jesus has spoken, "Let's go over to the other side," and the storm came so they doubted the Word of God. You must understand the purpose for the Storm. Storms were designed to take them under. Storms come to destroy you. Storm come so you can doubt the Word of God. But you must learn how to deal with your storm because Jesus is in your boat.

1 John 4:4 KJV

[4] Ye are of God, little children, and have overcome them: because greater is he that is in you, than he that is in the world.

You've got to learn how to deal with and speak to your storm.

And the disciples said, "Don't you care? Because the only time we find you sleeping is when I'm going through a storm."

But Jesus never answered them. He spoke to the wind and the water. He ignores the disciples and begins speaking to the thing that was trying to stop them. The thing that was trying to drown them, the thing that was trying to stop them from getting to the other side. The thing that was causing them to doubt and walk in disbelief.

You've got to come to a place where you talk to things that are trying to stop you. The prophetic dimension on your life is not to doubt or be afraid. It is not to cave in, it is not to give up. But you have to learn to speak to every storm. Jesus rebuked the storm. He spoke to the water and said be still. You must understand that everything God created has an ear. He said if you speak to the mountain and say, "be thou removed", the mountain will be moved. Why? Because the mountain has an ear. You have to learn how to speak to your bills and say you will be paid. Speak to your job and say I will get a raise, I will make six figures. Speak to the car and say you will drive and not break down. You have authority to speak to every cell in your body. You will not have cancer. Speak to your heart. You will not have a heart attack. Speak to the left side of your body. You will not have a stroke. Speak to your kidney. You will not be on dialysis. Speak to your lungs. My God you will not have any kind of breathing problem. Speak to your limbs. You will not be in a wheelchair. Speak to your bank account. You will not be in the red. You have to learn how to speak. Speak to your children and declare you will not be incarcerated. You will not go to jail. You will not do drugs. Speak to your marriage and declare there will be no argument and there will be no divorce. There will be no separation. There will be no extramarital affair, you got to Speak. Speak to your business. I will prosper. I will excel in business. I will be excellent.

Whatever I touch is blessed. Speak to your immigration. I will not be deported. I will be a citizen. Speak to your finances. I will prosper. I will excel, and money will know my name and my address. My income bracket will increase. Speak to your house. Increase the square footage of my house in the name of Jesus Christ. You have to learn how to speak. This storm will not take me under, but it's gonna take me over. I'm a child of the king. I'm the head and not the tail on the above and not beneath.

Jesus and the Disciples got to the other side. It will not take you under. It will take you over, but you have to learn how to speak.

Speak to your storm I'm not going under. I'm going over.

Isaiah 40:31 KJV

[31] But they that wait upon the Lord shall renew their strength; they shall mount up with wings as eagles; they shall run, and not be weary; and they shall walk, and not faint.

This storm not take you under, I see God taking you over In Jesus Mighty Name!!!

Made in the USA
Middletown, DE
04 September 2022

72174299R10055